In the Spirit of the Wolf
Brian Heinz

The
WOLVES

Brian J. Heinz · *pictures by* Bernie Fuchs

Ballyhoo BookWorks Inc. · Shoreham

For my editor and fellow lover of wolves, Diane Arico
B. J. H.

For Babe
B. F.

Published by Ballyhoo BookWorks
P. O. Box 534
Shoreham, NY 11786

Designed by Atha Tehon
Printed in China
First Edition
1 3 5 7 9 10 8 6 4 2

Library of Congress Cataloging-in-Publication Data
Heinz Brian J., 1946-
The wolves / Brian J. Heinz ; pictures by Bernie Fuchs
p. cm.
Summary: Recounts how a wolf pack struggles to survive
in the frozen North and includes an author's note describing the dwindling
wolf population in America and the threat of extinction.
Originally published: New York : Dial Books for Young Readers, c1996.
ISBN 0-936335-11-4 (alk. paper)
1. Wolves-Juvenile literature. 2. Wolves-Behavior-Juvenile literature.
I. Fuchs, Bernie, ill. II. Title
QL737.C22H43   2005   599.773--dc22

The illustrations were done in oils on canvas.

For hundreds of years, when Native Americans were the only inhabitants of our continent, tens of thousands of wolves roamed freely over all of North America. These magnificent animals played an important role in ecology, controlling the large populations of herd animals.

As America was settled by white Europeans, our human population grew quickly and spread across the continent. Land was cleared for farming, ranching, timber harvesting, and mining. The natural habitat of wolves was destroyed and their numbers declined rapidly.

There is no documented evidence of wolves attacking people in the wild, yet they were seen as a threat to humankind. For decades wolves were continually hunted, poisoned, and trapped to collect a bounty, or payment, for their pelts. Now fewer than 1,700 wolves are found only in areas of northern Minnesota, Wisconsin, and Michigan, and just a few dozen animals remain in isolated areas of the American West. The Rocky Mountain Gray Wolf is currently listed as "endangered" under the U.S. Endangered Species Act.

The wolf populations in Alaska (about 7,000) and Canada (about 50,000) are presently at healthy numbers, and environmental organizations, with support from the United States government, have reintroduced wolves into some of our western national parks. Breeding programs are also underway for endangered species like the Mexican Red Wolf, with plans to return populations to the American Southwest.

To save these magnificent animals will take more than repopulation programs, for the real enemy of the wolf is ignorance. By learning more about the true nature of wolves and wiping away the myths that many people still hold in their minds, a new picture of the wolf can emerge.

B. J. H.

The mountains ache with a deep chill, and their rugged shoulders huddle over the valley below. A gray cloud creeps over the peaks and rolls slowly, hugging the ground, down the slopes.

The cloud is deep and heavy, miles across, as it pushes its way past the timberline of lodgepole pines. In twisted, heaving swirls, it carries a thousand tons of snow.

And it carries the wolves.

Pahtoo leads the pack in shaggy fur the color of chimney soot. But beneath his dense winter coat his great body is rangy and rawboned, and his ribs push out against his lean sides.

Behind Pahtoo the faces of a dozen wolves peer from the storm cloud's edge like ghosts beneath a veil. Their sunken bellies and bony haunches tell the story. It is a savage winter in a wild land, and the pack has not eaten in three days. Survival depends upon Pahtoo's intelligence, his skills, his instincts.

And it depends upon the elk.

Pahtoo has shadowed the elks' trail for twenty miles, following droppings and the scent of hoofprints. Finally he has found the herd grazing far below.

The wind moans into the valley while Pahtoo's amber eyes watch a bull elk kick at the earth, roll his muscled neck, and snort a short whistle.

The other elk raise their heads from sparse grasses they've uncovered under the crust of earlier snows. Their brown bodies stand frozen, silent. Unblinking eyes gaze up the mountainside. The elk herd gathers together in a loose string behind the bull and moves to the east.

Pahtoo studies the elk. The pack waits and the snow begins to fall. The snow is furious, dizzy, tumbling down in huge flakes. In only moments the pine boughs bend under thick, white topcoats. The snow clings in wet collars to the dense manes around the wolves' necks. It settles over their brows and dusts their muzzles. But for their eyes and black noses, the wolves appear to have vanished.

Pahtoo lowers his head and steps forward. The pack watches, following the silent commands of his body movements. They shake away the snow. Lean sides heave and fall as clouds of moist breath billow from their nostrils. Tails twitch. Pahtoo signals the pack's advance in a low, throaty howl, and the wolves move like smoke down the mountain.

Pahtoo's lifelong mate, Nikki, moves up beside him, her white face encircled by pale gray fur. If she is here to see the spring, she will carry Pahtoo's pups. Pahtoo nuzzles her cheek as their eyes meet, but both know there is work to be done if the pack is to survive the winter.

Several young males and a few females make up the rest of the pack.
And for some of the yearlings, this is their first major hunt. They will
depend on Pahtoo's leadership. Now, driven by a hollow hunger, the wolves
stream into the valley.

Pahtoo quickens the pace and closes ground on the elk. The valley resounds in a chorus of excited barks. With tails erect as banners in battle, the wolves break into a run and fan out on both sides of the elk like a band of commandos. Pahtoo has trained them well.

The wolves' mouths are open, panting, pulling icy air into their lungs. They lunge and snarl, baring powerful, two-inch canines.

Pahtoo cuts across the path of the large bull. The elk stands his ground and thrusts at the wolf with a deadly rack of antlers. Backed by eight-hundred pounds of body weight and years of experience, the antler points carve vicious lines through the air again and again.

Pahtoo springs away and races forward. It is a game. A test. He knows this is not their quarry. This elk is too quick, too strong. And the pack leader remembers the raking scars across his ribs, scars of his youth, his learning years, from past encounters with the elk. No, this is not the one.

The trial continues. Trotting on their toes through the snow, the wolves ignore their weary, aching muscles and weave through the elk, testing each member of the herd. They keep the elk running and confused as they look for faltering steps that identify the weak, the old, the sick.

Two young wolves join Pahtoo and Nikki. The group surrounds a large female elk, taking turns to rush at her hindquarters. But she is strong and quick and lashes out with hooves that could tear open the belly of a careless wolf.

A yearling wolf moves in on her right and is sent reeling by a sudden kick to his loins. He tumbles through the snow, yelping, and limps away. He will learn. But Pahtoo knows this is not their elk.

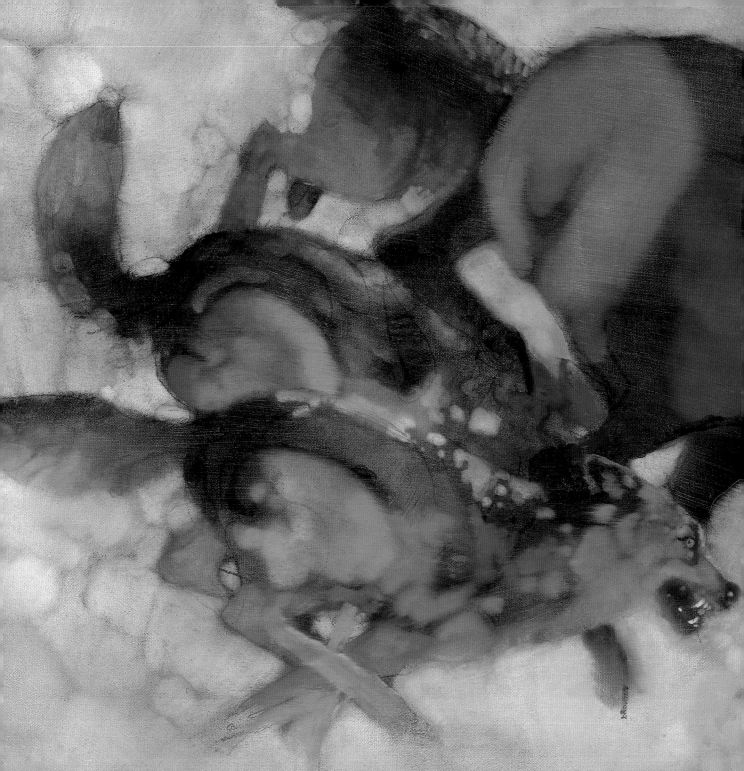

Three wolves have cut an old female off from the herd. She is heavy and slow. *This* is the elk. Exhausted and sick, she would never have lived to see the spring. As the wolves single her out, they become strange allies to the remaining elk, for she has slowed down the herd and eaten valuable grasses best left for the healthy and strong. Her time was chosen not by the wolves, but by the brutal winter and this harsh land.

The wolves call out in frenzied, hooting barks that unite the pack around the old elk as they leave the herd to move on in peace.

The wolves work as a team. Circling the elk, they guide her into deeper snow at the forest's edge. She stumbles under shaky steps and mucus clogs her wheezing snout. In her end is a new beginning for Pahtoo and his pack.

Pahtoo and Nikki distract the elk as others rush in one by one, from the right, the left, the rear. The wolves strike and move away. Pahtoo's jaws close with a crippling snap on her hamstring. Nikki clamps her teeth around the elk's muzzle, and she is taken down. It is over.

As leaders, Pahtoo and Nikki are first at the kill. Other pack members spread over the carcass, each claiming their spot with defensive snarls.

The youngest wolves must wait their turn. But there is food enough for
all, and it will keep the pack strong for many days. The snowfall is over,
and ravens are huddled in the treetops to await their scraps.

After the wolves have eaten, they move into the woods and settle down to grooming. They clean their fur and bite away at the painful ice that has lodged between the pads of their feet. With bellies full, life in the pack becomes less serious.

One young wolf grabs a short branch between his teeth and shakes it in the face of Pahtoo. It is a teasing invitation to play. In moments the clan of wolves is kicking up snow, racing after one another in a spirited game of "pass the stick." The faces of the wolves are alive with joy. It is a romping free-for-all and everyone plays.

Later the wolf clan rests, piled loosely against one another and wrapping bushy tails around their noses for warmth. Pahtoo lies with his great head across Nikki's neck, but his eyes remain open. For the moment there is peace and contentment. Pahtoo has proven his leadership, raising the pack's chances of survival.

The sky is clear and dark, speckled with countless stars. The woods are lit by a waxing moon and Pahtoo rises. Moving to a high spot of ground, he arches his head back. His primitive howl rolls like a river through the valley.

Nikki moves in beside him. They are joined by the clan, and the song of the pack echoes in an eerie symphony from the mountains to the heavens.